Published by

James H. Kaster

Concord, NC

Printed in the United States of America

ISBN: 978-0-982-82202-9

The information contained within this book is true and complete to the best of my knowledge. Material was gathered from manufacturers' brochures, advertisements and media kits. Information is provided without any guarantee on the part of the publisher. Publisher also disclaims any liability incurred from use of this information.

© 2010 by James H. Kaster

All rights reserved. No part of this publication may be reproduced or transmitted in any form or by any means, electronic or mechanical, including photocopy, scanning, recording or any information retrieval system without permission in writing from the publisher. Permission is never granted for commercial purposes.

Manufacturer, vehicle, model, trim names and/or designations are the trademarks of the respective companies. They are used for identification purposes only. This is not an official publication of any of these companies or manufacturers.

Table of Contents

Table of Contents	2
Foreword	3
The 80's Measured	4
1980	5
1981	14
1982	23
1983	32
1984	38
1985	46
1986	53
1987	61
1988	68
1989	76
Index	84

Chapters are organized by year and then alphabetically by manufacturer within year. See the Index for a list of manufacturers within each year.

1986 Ford Taurus LX

Foreword

The 80's. Like many of the decades before it, it was a decade of change. As the disco era was coming to a close, the glamour cars representing that time were becoming obsolete. Over the 80's decade, the industry began phasing out vinyl roofs, opera windows, opera lights, velour upholstery and other remnants of glitz. (Although pillow-type seats remained very popular in upper level trim cars.) Consumers demanded more function and feedback from their cars. As a result, cars became more driver-oriented, without sacrificing comfort.

The 80's. Unlike, the times before, however, it was a time when lines blurred even more. Re-badged, foreign assembled vehicles were sold on domestic car lots. Were cars considered "domestic" based on their assembly point or their content of U.S. made components? Did it matter as long as the profits went to a U.S. globally headquartered corporation? This debate still continues today.

Much like the blurring line of domestic/foreign definitions was the blurring of vehicle lines. In this decade we saw the introduction of the minivan with the Dodge Caravan/Plymouth Voyager and the introduction of the SUV by Jeep Cherokee. Though the manufacturers classified these vehicles as light trucks, they were used mostly by families with needs to haul people and their "stuff", replacing the role of the station wagon.

Trends in society found their ways into automobiles. Video game consoles became more popular and personal computers began appearing on household desks. A great use of electronics permeated in cars from controlling various mechanical systems to displaying instrumentation in digital readouts and even warning systems that talked.

The economy and a second gas crisis also had a significant impact, shaping manufacturers' responses throughout the 80's. Cars shrank in size and engine displacements. Many platforms migrated to front-wheel drive. And with a few years of experience building smaller cars, auto companies learned how to make smaller engines more powerful through an increased use of turbo-charging.

Yet, in the 80's, there were some contrasts. While cars continued to downsize and follow function, hairstyles grew. Women wore large, frizzy, crimped and messy styles while men wore mullets (business in the front, party in the back).

I began the 80's in college, studying computer science. Secretly, I pondered whether I should have considered more seriously a career in the automotive industry. There was just something about automobiles that kept my focus. Yet, my interest in computer technology proved equally strong. While software applications became a career, automobiles would become my passion.

The 80's, like 2008-2010 (the time of this composition) was a time of economic strife that threatens the survival of the U.S. auto industry. We find that Chrysler's survival, yet again, depends on government intervention. Yet, the struggle for the industry goes beyond Chrysler. GM is on life support, also using taxpayer money to rebuild. Chrysler survived the 80's and came out a stronger, more profitable corporation. It is yet to be seen if the same scenario holds true for Chrysler and GM as the economy of the Great Recession recovers.

As a young boy, my father inspired my passion for automobiles. We spent Sundays (there were blue laws then) on car lots, free from salespeople. We looked at cars, considered their styles, materials, features and options. We compared and noted other manufacturer's comparable vehicles to each car we studied. There was something we could find to appreciate in a base Pinto as well as the top of the line Lincoln. It wasn't about horsepower. For us, it was about the artistry of design, the folds and creases in the metal, styling cues that paid loyal homage to previous generations, extra comforts and conveniences, appointments and new technologies.

Today, my modest collection of cars include four cars from the 80's: the last year of the Lincoln Versailles, a Mercury Cougar XR-7, a Chrysler LeBaron Mark Cross convertible and a Chrysler LeBaron Mark Cross turbo coupe. I delight in driving them as they are now unique on the roads and reliable for everyday driving.

I hope you enjoy this trip through the 80's memory lane as much as I enjoy compiling the material.

James H. Kaster

The 80's Measured

The chart below shows the pattern of costs for various items throughout the decade. While the cost of bread was increasing, the cost of gasoline was decreasing and by the middle of the decade, a loaf of bread cost more than a gallon of gasoline. Housing prices made a big jump in 1989. Together, these two metrics ushered in the 90's SUV craze. Homeowners, using their newfound equity, took out second mortgages to purchase larger cars and SUVs than had been available in the 80's. With gas prices so low, the MPG concerns that started the early 80's recession was no longer a concern by the end of the decade. Interestingly, as we enter the 2010 & 2011 model years, we find ourselves in a similar, if not worse, predicament. The U.S. is in its most severe recession since World War II and the volatile cost of gasoline has consumers demanding fuel efficient vehicles. History is repeating.

Cost Comparison Chart

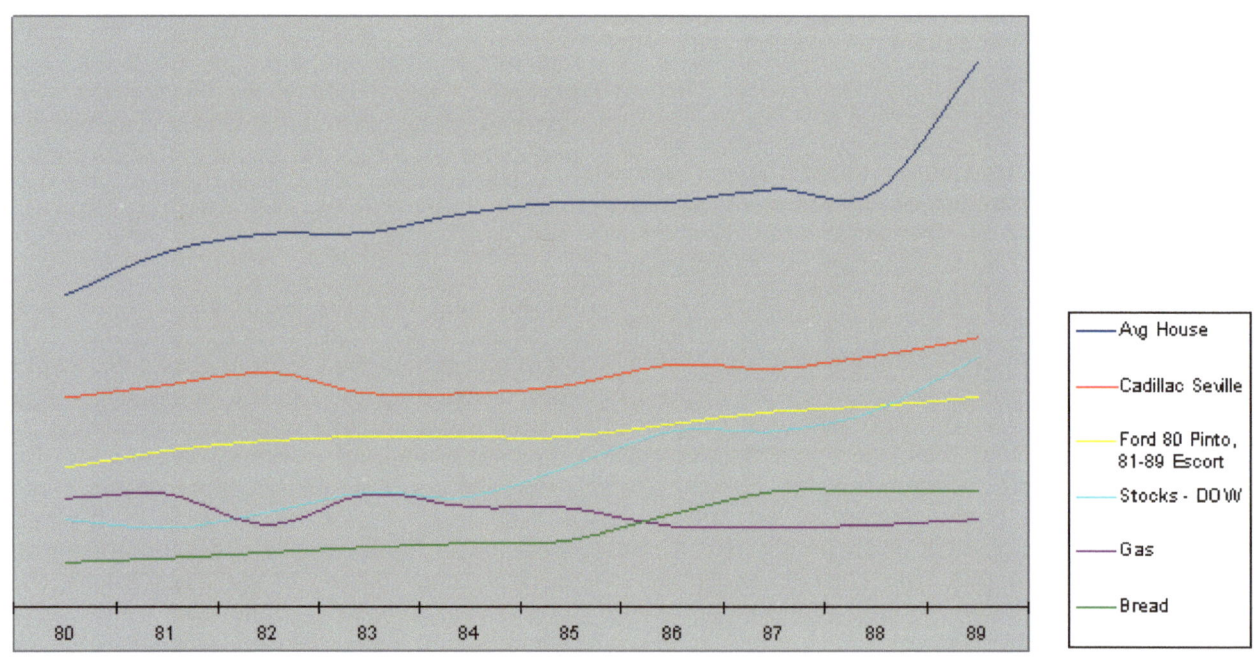

Percentage of change, comparing 1989 to 1980

Average House Price	74.7%
Cadillac Seville	29.1%
Ford '89 Escort / '80 Pinto	51.2%
Stocks – DOW	185.0%
Gallon of Gas	-18.5%
Loaf of Bread	168.6%

1980

1980 - Facts at Glance

News Headlines

- US operation failed to free hostages in Iran
- Ronald Reagan elected President
- Mount St. Helen Erupts
- John Lennon is killed
- Fire destroys MGM Grand Hotel in Las Vegas
- Winter Olympics held in Lake Placid
- Pac-Man introduced

Tops in Pop Culture

Music
- Call Me, Blondie

Movies
- Star Wars Episode V: The Empire Strikes Back

TV Show
- Dallas

Sports Champions

Basketball
- LA Lakers

Football
- Pittsburg Steelers

Baseball
- Philadelphia Phillies

MT – Car of the Year

Chevrolet Citation

1980 - FORD

New Model: 1980 Ford Thunderbird Silvery Anniversary

1980 Ford Thunderbird optional electronic instrument panel

1980 Ford Thunderbird Interior Luxury Group with leather

New 4.2 V8 engine & new 4-speed automatic overdrive for 5.0 engine only option

New Model: 1980 Ford Thunderbird with Exterior Luxury Group

1980 trim series:
Thunderbird
Silver Anniversary
Town Landau
Exterior & Interior Luxury
Exterior & Interior Decor
Standard Exterior & Interior

Granada engine choices: 4.1 liter inline 6-cylinder, 4.2 & 5.0 liter V8s

Last Model Run: 1980 Ford Granada Ghia 4-door Sedan

3 trim series: Granada, Granada Ghia, Granada ESS

1980 Ford Granada optional leather bucket seats

Granada ESS

Standard power team 2.3 liter OHC 4-cylinder w/4-speed manual

1980 Ford Fairmont Ghia 4-door

2.3 liter turbo 4-cylinder

1980 Ford Fairmont Futura Ghia Turbocharger

1980 Ford Fairmont Wagon

Ghia luxury steering wheel with fingertip speed control

1980 Ford Fairmont dash panel

Ghia flight bench seat in new luxury velour cloth

1980 Ford Fairmont Futura interior

1980 Ford LTD 4-door

5.8 liter V8 is optional

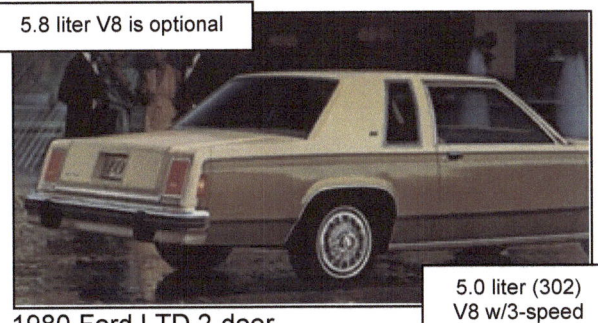

1980 Ford LTD 2-door

5.0 liter (302) V8 w/3-speed automatic are standard

Optional 4-speed AOD

Those 80s Cars - Ford

Mustang engines: 2.3 liter 4-cylinder, 2.3 turbo, 3.3 liter inline 6 & 4.2 liter V8

1980 Ford Mustang 3-Door Turbocharger (2.3 liter) with Michelin TRX tires

1.6 liter OHV 4-cylinder w/4-speed manual are standard

Last Model Run: 1980 Ford Fiesta with Décor Group option

1980 Ford Mustang hood scoop & new for 1980: Recaro Seats

1980 Ford Fiesta & Ghia interior

2.3 liter OHC 4-cylinder w/4-speed manual are standard

Last Model Run: 1980 Ford Pinto interior, Wagon & 2.3 liter OHC 4-cylinder engine

Pinto Models:
2-door sedan
3-door Runabouts
2-door wagons

Last Model Run: 1980 Ford Pinto 3-Door Runabout with Exterior Décor Group Option

1980 - LINCOLN

5.0 liter V8 w/3-speed auto

Last Model Run: 1980 Lincoln Versailles

Last Model Run: 1980 Lincoln Versailles

New Twin Comfort Lounge Seats replace last year's flight bench seat

1980 Lincoln Versailles standard Twin Comfort Lounge Seat cloth interior

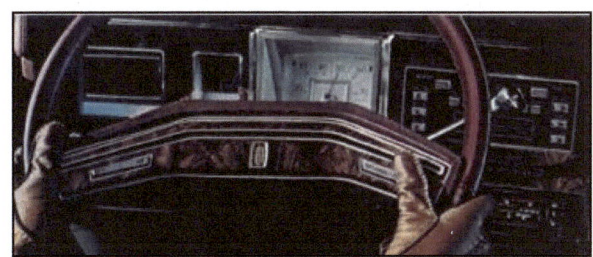

1980 Lincoln Versailles instrument panel

1980 Lincoln Versailles optional leather bucket seat interior

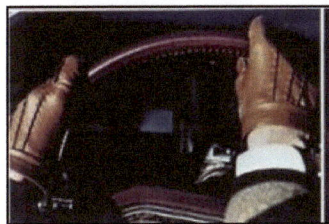

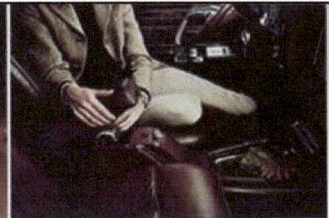

5.0 & 5.8 liter V8s with new 4-speed AOD

New Model: 1980 Lincoln Continental Coupe

1980 Lincoln Town Car interior

New Model: 1980 Lincoln Continental Town Car

New Model: 1980 Lincoln Continental Town Car

New Model: 1980 Lincoln Continental Mark VI Signature Series

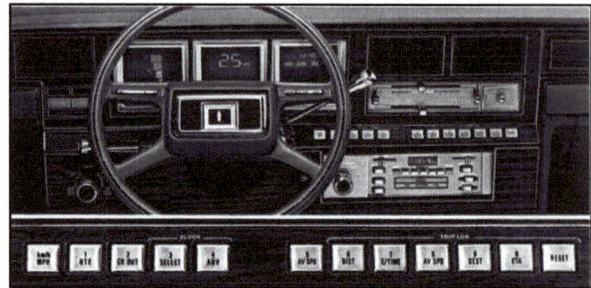
1980 Lincoln Continental Mark VI instrument panel

1980 Lincoln Continental Mark VI Signature Series 2-door interior

New Model: 1980 Lincoln Continental Mark VI Bill Blass Designer Series

1980 - MERCURY

Last Model Run: 1980 Mercury Monarch Ghia 4-door

Last Model Run: 1980 Mercury Monarch 2-door with ESS option

Monarch power team choices:
4.1 liter inline 6-cylinder, 4.2 & 5.0 liter V8
4-speed manual overdrive & 3-speed automatic

1980 Mercury Monarch flight bench with optional luxury cloth

1980 Mercury Monarch options

Capri engines:
2.3 liter 4-cylinder, 2.3 turbo
3.3 liter inline 6, 4.2 liter V8

1980 Mercury Capri RS Turbo

2.3 liter 4-cylinder

Last Model Run: 1980 Mercury Bobcat with Sport Option

Press Kit: "With its blend of European styling and American performance, U.S.-built Capri was an instant hit in 1979. For 1980 Capri will generate more excitement with a new optional 4.2 liter (255 CID) V-8 engine and new powertrain combination matching the 2.3-liter turbocharged engine with an automatic transmission." – 1980 Mercury Capri

Press Kit: "The Sport Option --- another exciting new styling innovation --- will feature a front air dam, a rear spoiler, a special black two-tone paint/tape treatment, and distinctive lower bodyside tape-striping."
– 1980 Mercury Bobcat

1980 Mercury Zephyr Sports Instrumentation Group option

1980 Mercury Zephyr Interior Accent Group option

Zephyr engines:
2.3 liter 4-cylinder, 2.3 turbo
3.3 liter inline 6, 4.2 liter V8

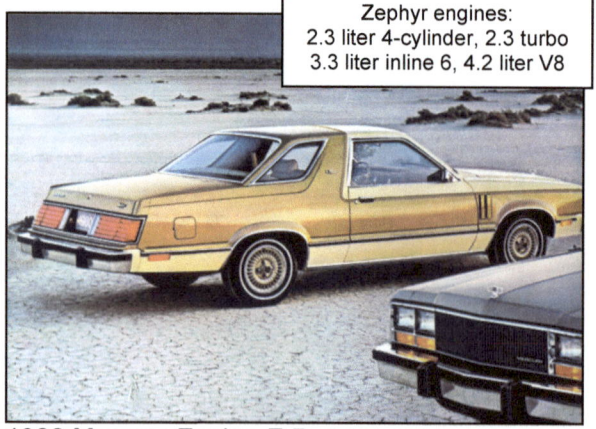

1980 Mercury Zephyr Z-7

1980 Mercury Zephyr 2-door with 2.3 Turbo

1980 Mercury Zephyr 2-door Sedan

Dual beam halogen headlamps are now standard

1980 Mercury Zephyr Station Wagon and Villager option

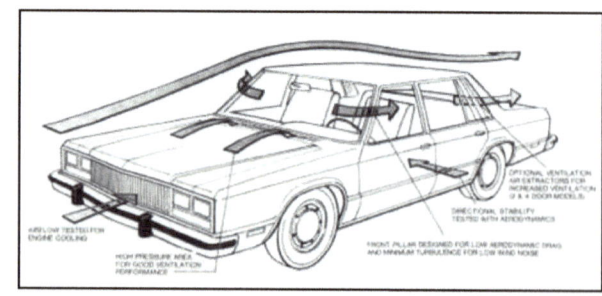

Those 80s Cars - Ford

4.2 & 5.0 liter V8s
3-speed auto & 4-speed AOD

New Model: 1980 Mercury Cougar XR-7

New Model: 1980 Mercury Cougar XR-7 with Luxury Group

1980 Mercury Cougar XR-7 Twin Comfort Lounge Seats

1980 Mercury Cougar XR-7 electronic dash

1980 Mercury Grand Marquis interior

1980 Mercury Cougar XR-7 Features & Options

5.0 & 5.8 liter V8s
3-speed auto & 4-speed AOD

New coach roof

1980 Mercury Grand Marquis 4-door Sedan

Those 80s Cars - Ford

1981

1981 - Facts at Glance

News Headlines

- Reagan fires striking air traffic controllers
- Researchers find the wreck of the Titanic
- Muhammad Ali retires
- Lady Diana marries Prince Charles
- Egyptian President Anwar Sadat is assassinated
- Sandra Day O'Connor appointed to Supreme Court
- 1st test tube baby is born
- Microsoft introduces MS-DOS
- MTV launched

Tops in Pop Culture

Music
- Bette Davis Eyes, Kim Carnes

Movies
- Raiders of the Lost Ark

TV Show
- Dallas

Sports Champions

Basketball
- Boston Celtics

Football
- Oakland Raiders

Baseball
- L.A. Dodgers

Motor Trend – Car of the Year

Chrysler K Cars:
Dodge Aries & Plymouth Reliant

1981 - FORD

1981 Ford Fairmont Futura 4-door Sedan

1981 Ford Fairmont 2-door Sedan

1981 Ford Fairmont Interior Luxury Group

1981 Ford Fairmont standard bucket seats

79.5 cu. ft. with rear seat folded

1981 Ford Fairmont Futura Squire Wagon

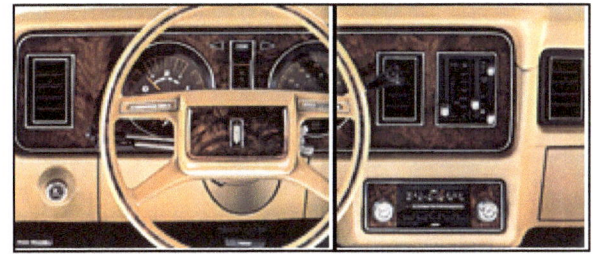
1981 Ford Fairmont instrument panel

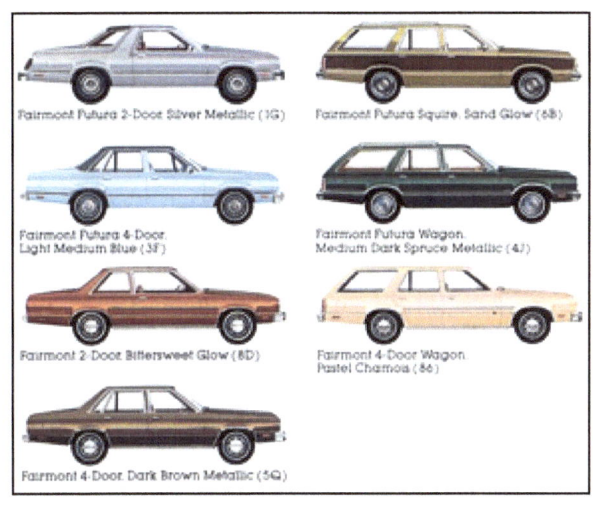

1.3 & 1.6 liter 4-cylinder engines

New Model: 1981 Ford Escort GLX 3-Door

New Model: 1981 Ford Escort GLX 4-door

From the Brochure: "Built to take on the world. Top Ford engineers from around the world teamed up to bring together the best of their better ideas. The result: Ford Escort. The new World Car. Escort is engineered for sure-footed traction with front wheel drive. Independent 4-wheel suspension. Rack and pinion steering precision. Plus new all-season steel-belted radial tires."
- 1981 Ford Escort

1981 Ford Escort GLX interior

2.3 liter 4-cylinder, 3.3 liter inline 6 & 4.2 liter V8 engines

New Model: 1981 Ford Granada GLX 2-door & GL 4-door

From the Brochure: "Built for a changing world. Introducing the Ford Granada for 1981, the newest entry in the modern field of American-built touring sedans. This is a totally redesigned Granada."   - 1981 Ford Granada

1981 Ford Granada instrument panel

1981 Ford Granada GLX split bench interior

3.3 liter inline 6 is new Thunderbird standard engine

1981 Ford Thunderbird Town Landau

1981 Ford Thunderbird with optional electronic instrument panel

1981 Ford LTD Crown Victoria 4-door Sedan

1981 Ford Thunderbird & Interior Luxury Group

1981 Ford LTD Crown Victoria interior

From the Brochure: "America's most popular sports car. Sporty good looks with sleek, aerodynamic lines and the exciting new T-Roof option."

- 1981 Ford Mustang

1981 Ford Mustang

Ford drops 5.0 liter V8 from Mustang, Granada & Fairmont

1981 Ford Mustang Ghia with new T-Roof option

Those 80s Cars - Ford

1981 - LINCOLN

5.8 liter V8 option is dropped

Last Model Run: 1981 Lincoln Town Car 2-door (only the 2-door is discontinued after 1981)

1981 Lincoln Town Car ("Continental" is dropped from the name this year)

1981 Lincoln Town Car 2-door leather interior

1981 Lincoln Town Car standard instrumentation

1981 Lincoln Town Car optional features

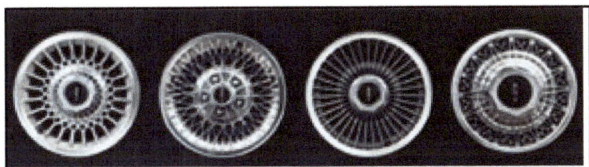

1981 Lincoln Continental Mark VI 4-door with standard electronic instrument panel

1981 Lincoln Continental Mark VI optional Luxury Group interior features

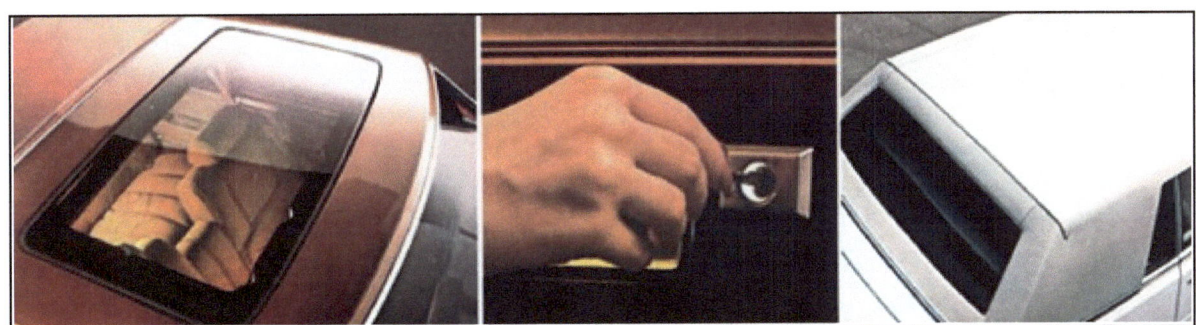

1981 Lincoln Continental Mark VI Bill Blass Designer Series

Those 80s Cars - Ford

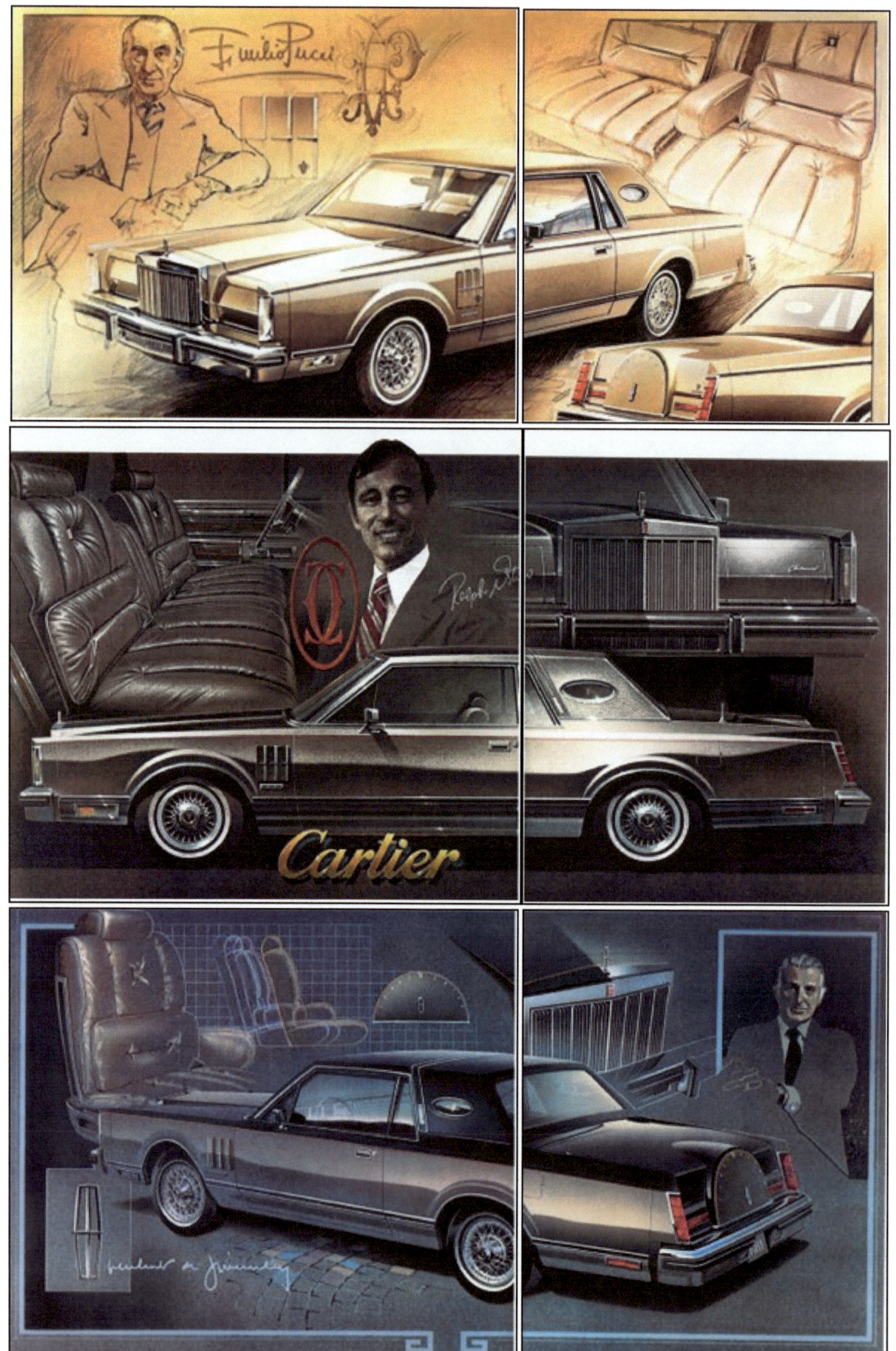

1981 Lincoln Continental Mark VI Pucci(top), Cartier(middle) and Givenchy(bottom) Designer Series

1981 - MERCURY

3.3 liter inline 6 is new Cougar XR-7 standard engine

1981 Mercury Cougar XR-7 GS

1981 Mercury Cougar XR-7 GS optional Recaro seat interior

1981 Mercury Cougar LS 4-door interior with optional leather

2.3 liter 4-cylinder, 3.3 liter inline 6 & 4.2 liter V8 engines

New Model: 1981 Mercury Cougar GS 4-door with optional Tu-Tone paint

New Model: 1981 Mercury Cougar 2-door with optional vinyl roof

1981 Mercury Grand Marquis

Those 80s Cars - Ford

1981 Mercury Capri, Black Magic edition shown at right

1981 Mercury Capri optional Black Magic interior

1.3 & 1.6 liter 4-cylinder engines
New Model: 1981 Mercury Lynx GS

New Model: 1981 Mercury Lynx GS Wagon

New Model: 1981 Mercury Lynx LS

1981 Mercury Lynx LS optional interior

1982

1982 - Facts at Glance

News Headlines	Tops in Pop Culture
- Falkland war ignites - USA Today launched - Disney's EPCOT center opens - 1st artificial heart transplanted - Vietnam Veterans Memorial dedicated	**Music** - Physical, Olivia Newton-John **Movies** - ET: The Extra-Terrestrial **TV Show** - 60 Minutes
Sports Champions	**Motor Trend – Car of the Year**
Basketball - L.A. Lakers **Football** - San Francisco 49ers **Baseball** - St. Louis Cardinals	 Chevrolet Camaro Z28

1982 - FORD

5.0 high output V8 optional

1982 Ford Mustang GLX Coupe

Last Model Run: 1982 Ford Thunderbird Heritage Series

1982 Ford Mustang GLX interior

New 3.8 liter V6 option

Last Model Run: 1982 Ford Thunderbird Heritage Series

1982 Ford Fairmont 2-door Coupe & interior

1982 Ford Thunderbird optional digital dash

1982 Ford Fairmont Futura 2-door Coupe

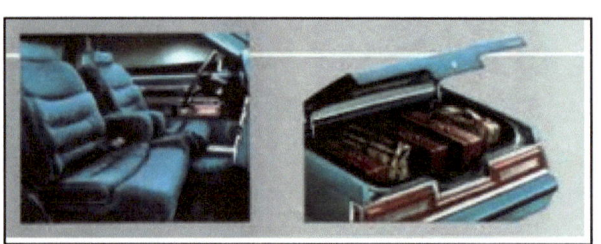

1982 Ford Thunderbird Heritage interior and deep-well trunk

1982 Ford Fairmont Futura Interior Luxury Group

1982 Ford Fairmont Futura 4-door Sedan

1982 Ford Escort 4-door GL Wagon (top left)
New Model & **Last Model Run:** 1982 Ford Granada GL Wagon (top right)
1982 Ford LTD Country Squire (bottom)

Last Model Run: 1982 Ford Granada GL 2-door Coupe

New 3.8 liter V6 option

New Model & **Last Model Run:** 1982 Ford Granada GL Wagon with Squire Option

1982 Ford Granada GL interior

Last Model Run: 1982 Ford Granada L 4-door Sedan

From the Brochure: "Quality is Job 1. At Ford Division, we believe our 1982 automobiles are the finest we have ever produced. This lineup of cars, from the sporty EXP to the elegant Thunderbird, with brand-new Escort 4-door Hatchback and Granada Wagon models, represents the latest in technology and Ford engineering achievement."
- 1982 Ford

1982 Ford Granada GLX instrument panel

5.8 liter V8 option is dropped

1982 Ford LTD Crown Victoria 4-door Sedan

LTD: 4-speed automatic overdrive transmission is standard

1982 Ford LTD Crown Victoria 2-door Coupe

LTD has over 22 cu. ft. of cargo space in its deep-well trunk

New Model: 1982 Ford Escort GL 4-door Hatchback

Escort outsold all import car lines in its first year

1982 Ford Escort GLX 2-door Hatchback

New Model: 1982 Ford EXP

1.6 liter 4-cylinder w/4-speed manual overdrive transaxle

New Model: 1982 Ford EXP

1982 Ford EXP optional shearling & leather

Those 80s Cars - Ford

1982 - LINCOLN

5.0 liter V8 with 4-speed automatic overdrive

New Model: 1982 Lincoln Continental

New Model: 1982 Lincoln Continental Givenchy Designer Series

New Model: 1982 Lincoln Continental Signature

1982 Lincoln Continental Givenchy Designer Series cloth interior

1982 Lincoln Continental instrument panel

From the Brochure: "Presenting the most original Continental since the original Continental. The new Continental for 1982. New in size, new in design, new in spirit, new in splendor. The most elegant Continental ever fashioned. But for all its contemporary character, Continental draws upon the rich traditions of the past... as in its formal rear-deck treatment."

- 1982 Lincoln Continental

1982 Lincoln Continental Mark VI Signature Series 2-door

1982 Lincoln Town Car Signature Series

1982 Lincoln Continental Mark VI Signature Series 4-door

1982 Lincoln Town Car Signature Series cloth interior

Lincoln Continental Mark VI Signature Series

From the Brochure: "Electronic Instrument Panel and Message Center. The stylish, easy-to-read Electronic Instrument Panel includes electronic digital speedometer, electronic graphic fuel gauge, month/day/date electronic clock. The Message Center includes trip log, warning messages and instantaneous fuel economy."

- 1982 Lincoln Town Car

1982 Lincoln Town Car dash with optional electronic instrument panel with message center

1982 Lincoln Town Car Signature Series

1982 - MERCURY

Last Model Run: 1982 Mercury Cougar XR-7 (GS trim level shown)

New 3.8 liter V6 option
5.0 liter V8 dropped

1982 Mercury Cougar XR-7 GS instrument panel

1982 Mercury Cougar XR-7 GS interior

New Model: 1982 Mercury Lynx LS 5-Door

1982 Mercury Lynx GL 3-Door

1982 Mercury Lynx LS interior

58.3 cu. ft. cargo space

1982 Mercury Lynx GS Wagon with Villager option (front) and GL Wagon (back)

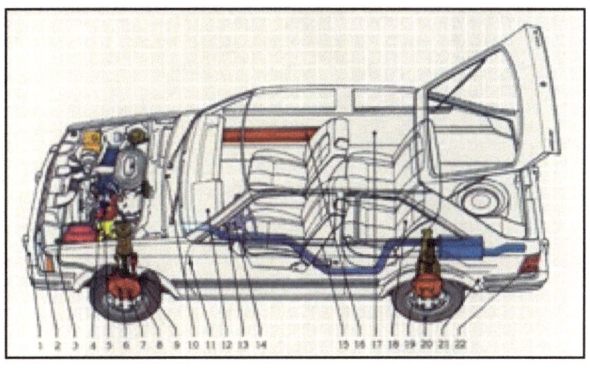

1.6 liter 4-cylinder w/4-speed manual overdrive transaxle

New Model: 1982 Mercury LN7

New Model: 1982 Mercury LN7

New Model: 1982 Mercury LN7

1982 Mercury LN7 interior

1982 Mercury LN7 instrument panel

From the Brochure: "LN7. Starting today, there is something beyond the fuel-efficient automobile. Come drive a road you've never traveled before. The new two-seater Mercury LN7 will change forever your ideas about what 'economy' means. It has 29 EPA estimated MPG, 46 estimated highway… along with stunning good looks and the best aerodynamic ratings of any standard-equipped American-built car. Engineered with some of the most advanced technology of our times… including front-wheel drive and a four-wheel independent suspension specially tuned for sport handling. And that translates into something that's been on the endangered species list until now, the fun driving. LN7: high style and high mileage… in a real driver's car."   – 1982 Mercury LN7

5.0 high output V8 optional

1982 Mercury Capri RS with T-Roof

1982 Mercury Capri optional Recaro interior

1982 Mercury Zephyr Z-7 GS

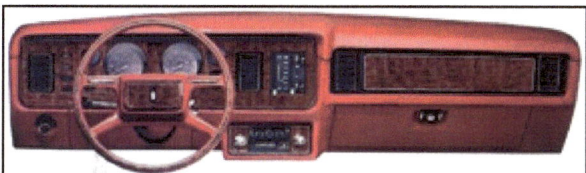
1982 Mercury Zephyr instrument panel

1982 Mercury Zephyr Z-7 GS interior

AM/FM Stereo 8-Track Tape Player

Last Model Run: 1982 Mercury Cougar LS 4-door Sedan

1982 Mercury Cougar LS interior

5.8 liter V8 option is dropped

1982 Mercury Grand Marquis 4-door Sedan

1982 Mercury Grand Marquis interior

1982 Mercury Zephyr GS 4-door Sedan

Those 80s Cars - Ford 31

1983

1983 - Facts at Glance

News Headlines

- Motorola introduces mobile phones in the United States
- Sally Ride becomes 1st American woamn in space
- IBM introduces PC XT
- MS Word & Lotus 1-2-3 are released
- Cabbage Patch Doll is introduced

Tops in Pop Culture

Music
- Every Breath You Take, The Police

Movies
- Star Wars Episode VI: Return of the Jedi

TV Show
- Dallas

Sports Champions

Basketball
- Philadelphia 76ers

Football
- Washington Redskins

Baseball
- Baltimore Orioles

Motor Trend – Car of the Year

AMC/Renault Alliance

1983 - FORD

1983 Ford product line-up
New Model: 1983 Ford LTD sedan (2nd from top)

New Model: 1983 Ford LTD Wagon

LTD engines: 2.3 liter 4-cylinder, 3.3 inline 6 & 3.8 liter V6

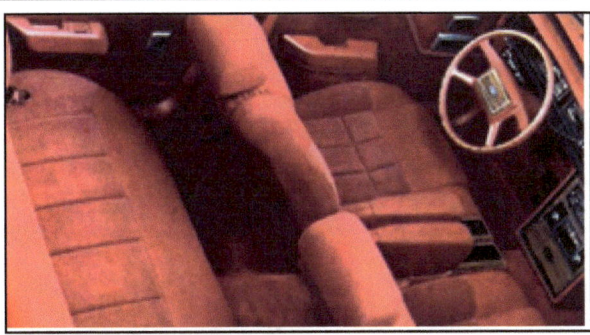
1983 Ford LTD interior

New options: EFI, 5-speed manual, TR-type wheels, handling suspension

1983 Ford Escort GT

1983 Ford LTD Crown Victoria 2-door Coupe

1983 Ford LTD Country Squire

1983 Ford LTD Country Squire

1983 Ford LTD Crown Victoria 2-door Coupe

1983 Ford Escort Wagon

New Model: 1983 Ford Thunderbird

Standard 3.8 liter V6
Optional 5.0 liter V8
.35 drag coefficient
New Model: 1983 Ford Thunderbird

1983 Ford Thunderbird interior

Refreshed: 1983 Ford Mustang GT

1983 Ford EXP

Refreshed: 1983 Ford Mustang GLX

Fairmont: the choice of over 1.3 million owners
Last Model Run: 1983 Ford Fairmont Futura

New: Mustang convertible
Refreshed: 1983 Ford Mustang line

1983 Ford Fairmont Futura interior

Last Model Run: 1983 Ford Fairmont Futura

Those 80s Cars - Ford

1983 - LINCOLN

1983 Lincoln Town Car Signature Series

Mark VI Signature Series interior

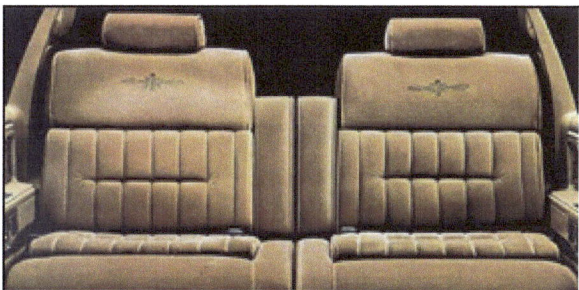
1983 Lincoln Town Car Signature Series interior

Last Model Run: 1983 Lincoln Continental Mark VI Signature Series 2-door Coupe

1983 Lincoln Continental

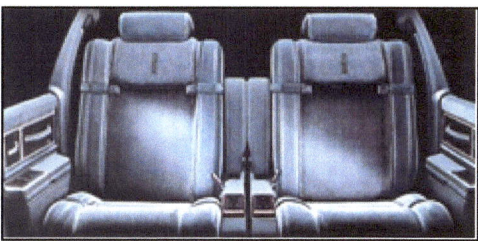

1983 - MERCURY

New Model: 1983 Mercury Cougar

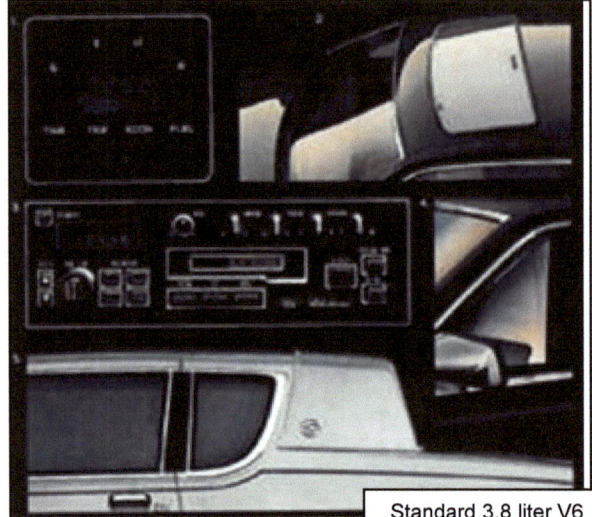
1983 Mercury Cougar options

Standard 3.8 liter V6
5.0 liter V8 optional

1983 Mercury Cougar LS interior

1983 Mercury Capri Black Magic, Capri L & GS

1983 Mercury Grand Marquis 4-door Sedan

With introduction of intermediate Marquis, all full-size models are now branded Grand Marquis

1983 Mercury Grand Marquis standard cloth interior

1983 Mercury Grand Marquis Colony Park Wagon

1983 Mercury Grand Marquis LS interior

Those 80s Cars - Ford

105.6" wheelbase

New Model: 1983 Mercury Marquis

New Model: 1983 Mercury Marquis Wagons

1983 Mercury Marquis optional interior

2.3 liter 4-cylinder & 3.3 liter inline 6

Last Model Run: 1983 Mercury Zephyr

1983 Mercury Lynx LS 5-Door

1983 Mercury Lynx GS 3-Door

1983 Mercury Lynx RS – 1.6 liter EFI 4-cylinder engine with 5-speed manual transmission and performance handling suspension are all standard equipment.

1983 Mercury Lynx LS interior

1983 Mercury LN7

1984

1984 - Facts at Glance

News Headlines

- Indria Ghandi is assassinated
- Summer Olympics held in LA
- French identify AIDS virus
- AT&T is broken up
- Apple Macintosh goes on sale
- CD players are introduced
- Michael Jackson's Thriller sells over 37 million copies

Tops in Pop Culture

Music
- When Doves Cry, Prince

Movies
- Ghost Busters

TV Show
- Dynasty

Sports Champions

Basketball
- Boston Celtics

Football
- L.A. Raiders

Baseball
- Detroit Tigers

Motor Trend – Car of the Year

Chevrolet Corvette

Those 80s Cars - Ford

1984 - FORD

2.3 liter EFI turbo, 145 hp at 4,600 RPM

1984 Ford Thunderbird Turbo Coupe

2.3 liter EFI turbo

New Series: 1984 Ford Mustang SVO

1984 Ford Thunderbird Turbo Coupe interior with optional leather

Thunderbird trim series: base, élan, FILA and Turbo Coupe

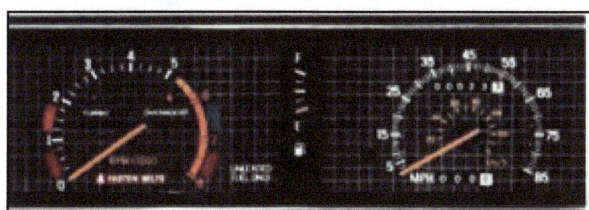

1984 Ford Thunderbird Turbo Coupe instrument panel

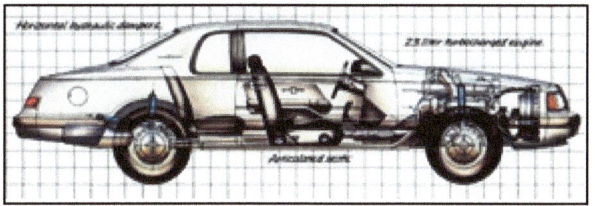

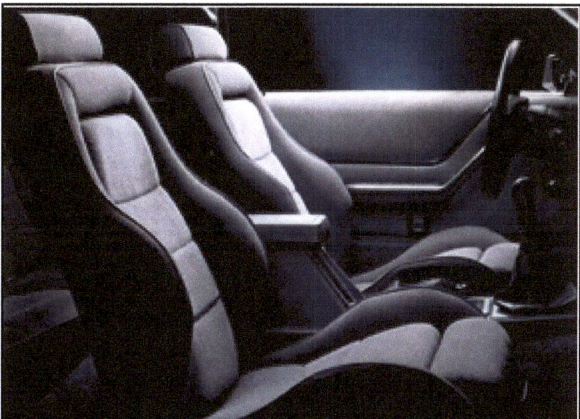

1984 Ford Mustang SVO interior

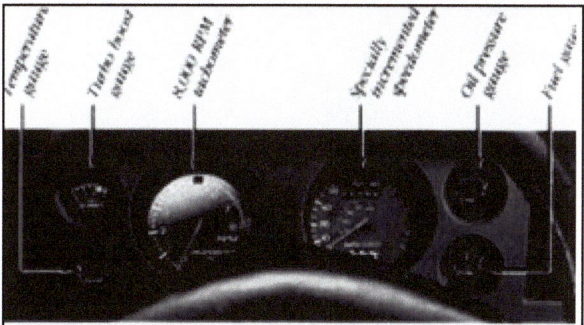

1984 Ford Mustang SVO instrument panel

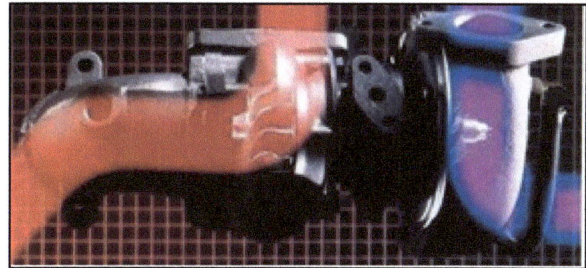

1984 Ford Escort LX Wagon

1984 Ford Escort GT instrument panel

1984 Ford Escort LX interior

1984 Ford Escort GL 4-door Hatchback

1.6 liter EFI turbo, 5-speed manual

1984 Ford Escort GT 2-door Hatchback

Standard 2.3 liter 4-cylinder

New Model: 1984 Ford Tempo GL 4-door Sedan

1984 Ford Tempo instrument panel

1984 Ford Tempo GL interior

2.0 liter diesel optional

New Model: 1984 Ford Tempo L 2-door Coupe

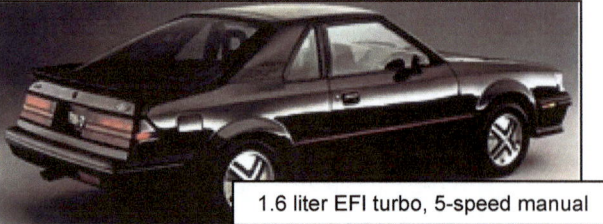
1.6 liter EFI turbo, 5-speed manual

1984 Ford EXP Turbo Coupe

1984 Ford EXP instrument panel

Those 80s Cars - Ford

1984 Ford LTD Wagon with optional bumper guards (left)
1984 LTD 4-door Sedan with optional styled road wheels (right)

1984 Ford LTD Crown Victoria interior with optional Interior Luxury Group leather seating surfaces and special sew style

1984 Ford LTD Brougham interior with optional leather seating surfaces and thick carpeting. Brougham comes standard with electronic digital clock, auto parking brake release, illuminated entry, dual illuminated vanity mirrors and Light Group.

LTD Crown Victoria wagons offers optional Dual Facing Rear Seats for 8-passenger seating and a standard 3-Way Magic Doorgate

1984 Ford LTD Country Squire Wagon

1984 Ford LTD Crown Victoria 4-door Sedan

1984 Ford LTD Crown Victoria 2-door Coupe

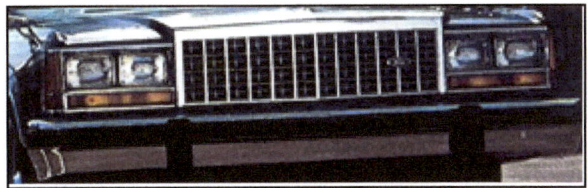

1984 Ford LTD Crown Victoria

1984 - LINCOLN

1984 Lincoln Town Car

1984 Lincoln Town Car Cartier

1984 Lincoln Town Car Cartier interior

1984 Lincoln Town Car

New Model: 1984 Lincoln VII LSC

Standard 5.0 liter EFI V8 with 4-speed automatic overdrive
2.4 liter turbocharged diesel, sourced by BMW, is optional

New Model: 1984 Lincoln VII LSC

1984 Lincoln VII LSC interior

.38 drag coefficient

New Model: 1984 Lincoln VII

Refreshed: 1984 Lincoln Continental

Refreshed: 1984 Lincoln Continental

Standard 5.0 liter EFI V8 with 4-speed automatic overdrive
2.4 liter turbocharged diesel, sourced by BMW, is optional

Refreshed: 1984 Lincoln Continental Valentino

1984 Lincoln Continental instrument panel & features

1984 Lincoln Continental interior

Refreshed: 1984 Lincoln Continental Givenchy

1984 - MERCURY

1984 Mercury Cougar XR-7 Turbo instruments

1984 Mercury Marquis Brougham

1984 Mercury Capri Turbo RS

1984 Mercury Capri Turbo RS interior

1984 Mercury Cougar XR-7 Turbo

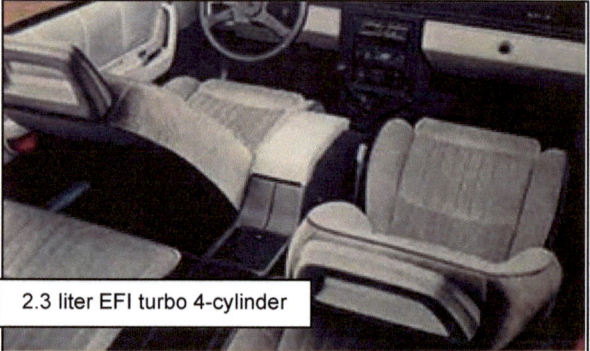

2.3 liter EFI turbo 4-cylinder

1984 Mercury Cougar XR-7 Turbo interior

1984 Mercury Grand Marquis

1984 Mercury Capri GS

1984 Mercury Capri roof options

AM/FM Stereo Cassette

1.6 liter EFI turbo, 5-speed manual

1984 Mercury Lynx LTS 4-door Hatchback

1984 Mercury Lynx GS interior

1984 Mercury Lynx Villager Wagon

1984 Mercury Lynx instrument panel

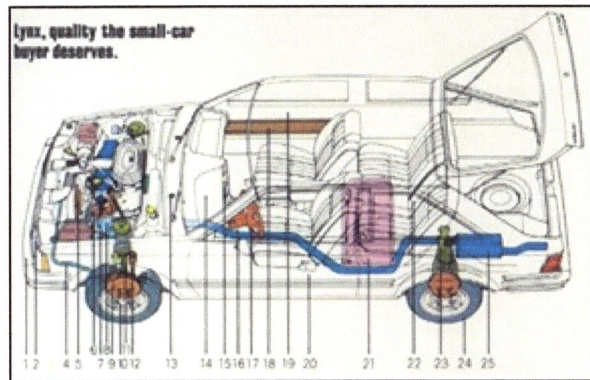

New Model: 1984 Mercury Topaz LS 4-door

Standard 2.3 liter 4-cylinder
Optional 2.0 liter 4-cylinder diesel

New Model: 1984 Mercury Topaz Sport 2-door

From the Brochure: "A more enlightened approach. There is a new kind of driver beginning to make an impact on the American scene. This more enlightened person shuns mere styling unsupported by substantial engineering. Mercury understands the message."
– 1984 Mercury Topaz

New Model: 1984 Mercury Topaz

1984 Mercury Topaz LS interior

1985

1985 - Facts at Glance

News Headlines

- Live Aid concert raises $50 million for famine relief in Ethiopia
- 8.1 earthquake hits Mexico City
- Boris Becker becomes the youngest player to win Wimbledon, at 17 years old

Tops in Pop Culture

Music
- Careless Whisper, Wham! Featuring George Michael

Movies
- Back to the Future

TV Show
- The Cosby Show

Sports Champions

Basketball
- L.A. Lakers

Football
- San Francisco 49ers

Baseball
- Kansas City Royals

Motor Trend – Car of the Year

Volkswagen GTI

Those 80s Cars - Ford

1985 - FORD

1985 Ford Mustang GT

Standard new articulated seats on the GT series

1985 Ford Mustang GT interior

1985 Ford Mustang instrument panel

Mustang 3.8 liter V6 optional on LX 2- & 3-door models; standard on LX convertible

Tempo GLX is available in standard and Luxury packages, each equipped with numerous comfort and convenience features.

Tempo GL comes in four new equipment packages: Standard, Select, Luxury and Sport. So anyone can enjoy GL's outstanding value.

Tempo L adds electronic fuel injection, new side window demisters and integral instrument panel storage shelf to its impressive list of features.

Mustang LX, in 2-door, 3-door and convertible models, is packed with extra value standard equipment. The 2-door also comes with a very attractive price.

Mustang LX Convertible combines the fine points of the 2-door with a power retractable top for true open air cruising.

Mustang GT 3-door and GT Convertible are excellent performers on all fronts. They have quick acceleration and firm suspensions for solid road holding capability.

1985½ Mustang SVO was developed by Ford Special Vehicle Operations group to set new standard in affordable grand touring cars. Higher performance and aero-designed headlamps head the list of new SVO features. For availability of the 1985½ SVO, see your Ford Dealer.

1985 Ford Tempo GLX interior

1985 Ford Tempo instrument panel

Tempo: New standard EFI on 2.3 liter 4-cylinder engine

1985 Ford EXP Luxury Coupe

1985 Ford Thunderbird FILA

New Thunderbird instrument panel for 1985

1985 Ford Thunderbird Turbo Coupe instruments

1985 Ford Thunderbird Turbo Coupe interior

1985 Ford LTD Crown Victoria 4-door Sedan

1985 Ford LTD Crown Victoria instrument panel

1985 Ford LTD Wagon with Squire Option

1985 Ford LTD Brougham instrument panel

1985 Ford LTD Brougham interior

1985 Ford LTD Brougham 4-door Sedan

New LTD LX model comes with 5.0 HO & modified handling

1985 Ford Escort LX 4-door Hatchback

Those 80s Cars - Ford

1985 - LINCOLN

Last year for diesel option

1985 Lincoln Mark VII LSC

From the Brochure: "The luxury line that offers the luxury of choice. In today's world, it is not enough for a luxury car to offer a plush interior and a quiet ride. Real-world driving conditions dictate that the modern luxury automobile provide other 'luxuries' as well. Safe and responsive handling, poise under the worst conditions, and a passenger compartment that is not only elegant, but also spacious, functional and convenient – these are necessities in today's luxury automobile. There are certain intangible luxuries, too: quality workmanship, value, and not the least, the sheer joy of driving."
— 1985 Lincoln

1985 Lincoln Continental

New grille & tail lamps

1985 Lincoln Town Car

1985 - MERCURY

1985 Mercury Capri interior

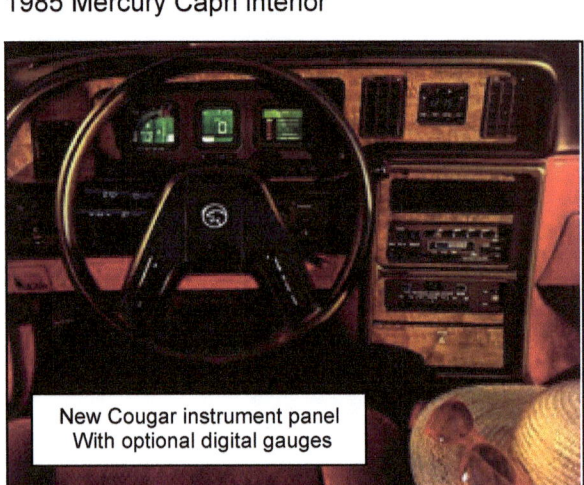
New Cougar instrument panel
With optional digital gauges

1985 Mercury Cougar digital instrument panel

1985 Mercury Grand Marquis & Colony Park

1985 Mercury Grand Marquis LS4-door Sedan

1985 Mercury Capri RS

Capri RS: standard 5.0 liter High-Output V8, 4-bbl carburetor and 5-speed overdrive manual gearbox

2.3 liter turbo 4-cylinder standard on XR-7 series

1985 Mercury Cougar XR-7

Engine choices: 3.8 V6 & 5.0 V8

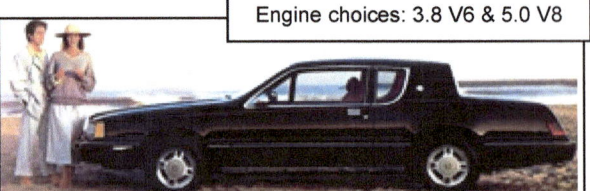
1985 Mercury Cougar LS

1985 Mercury Grand Marquis LS interior

Those 80s Cars - Ford

New standard EFI on 2.3 liter

1985 Mercury Topaz LS

1985 Mercury Lynx Wagon

1985 Mercury Topaz LS interior

1985 Mercury Lynx GS interior

1985 Mercury Lynx GS 4-door Hatchback

1985 Mercury Marquis Brougham

1985 Mercury Marquis Wagons

1985 Mercury Marquis interior

1985 - MERKUR

.33 drag coefficient

New Model: 1985 Merkur XR4Ti

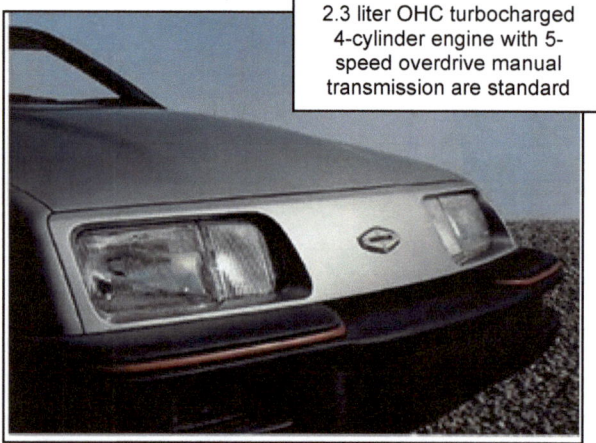

2.3 liter OHC turbocharged 4-cylinder engine with 5-speed overdrive manual transmission are standard

New Model: 1985 Merkur XR4Ti

1985 Merkur XR4Ti instrument panel

1985 Merkur XR4Ti interior

175 horsepower
200 lb. ft. torque

MERKUR XR4TI FROM GERMANY. PERFORMANCE THAT GOES BEYOND MERE STATISTICS.

1986

1986 - Facts at Glance

News Headlines

- SALT signed
- Chernobyl nuclear accident
- Iran-Contra Affair begins
- Mike Tyson becomes youngest heavyweight champion
- UK & France announce plans for Channel Tunnel
- Shuttle Challenger disaster

Tops in Pop Culture

Music
- That's What Friends Are For, Dionne & Friends

Movies
- Top Gun

TV Show
- The Cosby Show

Sports Champions

Basketball
- Boston Celtics

Football
- Chicago Bears

Baseball
- N.Y. Mets

Motor Trend – Car of the Year

Ford Taurus LX

1986 - FORD

A new 2.5 liter 4-cylinder is offered with a 3-speed auto or 5-speed manual. Most, are sold with a 3.0 liter multiple-port fuel-injected V6 & 4-speed auto overdrive.

New Model: 1986 Ford Taurus LX

1986 Ford Taurus GL interior

New Model: 1986 Ford Taurus LX Wagon

From the Brochure: "The 1986 Ford Taurus, *Motor Trend* Car of the Year, represents a remarkable combination of advanced design, interior roominess and all-around performance. It invites comparison to *any* car in the world today because its five years of planning were based on a 'best in class' philosophy."
- 1986 Ford Taurus

1986 Ford LTD Crown Victoria LX 4-door Sedan

1986 Ford LTD Crown Victoria LX interior

Those 80s Cars - Ford

1986 Ford LTD Country Squire Wagon

Last Model Run: 1986 Ford LTD

Last Model Run: 1986 Ford LTD

1986 Ford Thunderbird

1986 Ford Thunderbird élan interior

1986 Ford LTD Crown Victoria instrument panel

1986 Ford LTD Crown Victoria 2-door Coupe

1986 Ford Mustang 2-door Sedan

1986 Ford Mustang GT interior

From the Brochure: "Sporty, spirited Ford Mustang model choices begin with the LX 2-door sedan, 2-door hatchback or convertible. Next is breathtaking performance: GT 2-door hatchback or convertible. Finally there's the sophistication of Mustang SVO."
- 1986 Ford Mustang

1986 Ford Escort LX 4-door Hatchback

New Escort engine: 1.9 liter 4-cylinder
Diesel engine dropped

1986 Ford Escort LX Wagon

1.9 liter 4-cylinder

Refreshed: 1986 Ford EXP Luxury Coupe

1986 Ford Escort LX interior

1986 Ford EXP Luxury Coupe interior

New Model: 1986 Ford Aerostar (Though truck based, unlike the Chrysler minivans, this was Ford's response to Chrysler's leading design.)

1986 Ford Tempo LX 2-door Coupe

1986 Ford Aerostar interior

Seating up to 7-passengers & cargo space up to 139.2 cu. ft.
2.3 liter EFI 4-cylinder standard with 2.8 liter V6 optional

1986 Ford Tempo LX interior

Those 80s Cars - Ford

1986 - LINCOLN

1986 Lincoln Mark VII LSC

1986 Lincoln Mark VII LSC interior

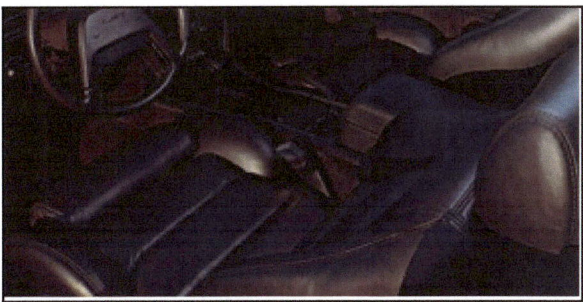
1986 Lincoln Mark VII LSC interior

3 trim series: Mark VII, Bill Blass, LSC

1986 Lincoln Continental

2 trim series: Continental & Givenchy

1986 Lincoln Town Car

3 trim series: Town Car, Signature & Cartier

1986 - MERCURY

A new 2.5 liter 4-cylinder & 3.0 liter V6 engines

New Model: 1986 Mercury Sable LS Sedan

From the Brochure: "Sable is designed to change the way you think about contemporary automobiles. The new Mercury Sable is a sophisticated shape that blends contemporary style and efficient performance in the manner of great a European road car.

Sable was designed to fulfill the needs of today's discriminating buyer – spaciousness, comfort and superior driving characteristics."
— 1986 Mercury Sable

New Model: 1986 Mercury LS Wagon

Last Model Run: 1986 Mercury Marquis

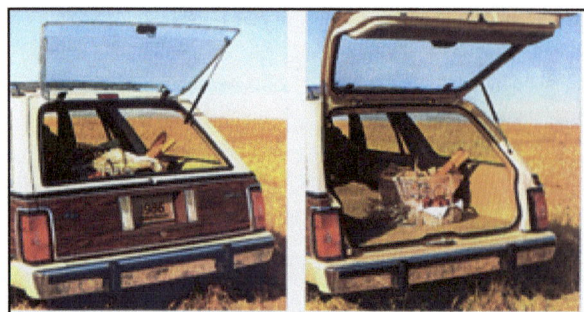

Last Model Run: 1986 Mercury Marquis Wagon

1986 Mercury Sable LS interior

1986 Mercury Marquis interior

From the Brochure: "Cougar XR-7 proves that a car can be strong on performance without being musclebound. The Cougar XR-7 is designed to use the wind to achieve practical, functional benefits."
— 1986 Mercury Cougar XR-7

1986 Mercury Cougar XR-7

1986 Mercury Cougar LS interior

1986 Mercury Topaz GS

1986 Mercury Topaz interior

Last Model Run: 1986 Mercury Capri

1986 Mercury Capri RS interior

Capri RS: 0 – 50 in under 6 seconds

Last Model Run: 1986 Mercury Capri RS 5.0

1986 Mercury Lynx XR3 interior

Those 80s Cars - Ford

1986 Mercury Grand Marquis LS Sedan

1986 Mercury Grand Marquis Coupe & Colony Park Wagon

1986 Mercury Lynx GS Wagon

New Series: 1986 Mercury Lynx XR3

XR3 sports a new 1.9 liter EFI 4-cylinder engine, 15" aluminum wheels, fog lamps, front air dam, rear spoiler, special wheel spats and rocker panel moldings

1986 Mercury Grand Marquis LS interior

1986 - MERKUR

1986 Merkur XR4Ti (same as 1985)

Those 80s Cars - Ford

1987

1987- Facts at Glance

News Headlines

- Oct 19 Stock Market crashes $508, dropping 22.6%
- Fox broadcasting debuts
- Televangelist Jim Bakker scandal breaks

Tops in Pop Culture

Music
- Walk Like an Egyptian, Bangles

Movies
- 3 Men and a Baby

TV Show
- The Cosby Show

Sports Champions

Basketball
- L.A. Lakers

Football
- N.Y. Giants

Baseball
- Minnesota Twins

Motor Trend – Car of the Year

Ford Thunderbird Turbo Coupe

1987 - FORD

Refreshed: 1987 Ford Mustang GT

New interior

1987 Ford Mustang LX interior with new dash

1987 Ford Mustang LX Coupe

1987 Ford Mustang Cobra GT Convertible

Cobra GT: 225 hp at 4,000 RPM
300 lb./ft. torque at 3,200 RPM

Refreshed: 1987 Ford Thunderbird LX

1987 Ford Thunderbird optional electronic instrument cluster

1987 Ford Thunderbird LX interior

New 2.3 turbo intercooled rated at 190 hp

Refreshed: 1987 Ford Thunderbird Turbo Coupe

Those 80s Cars - Ford

1987 Ford Taurus LX Sedan & Wagon

1987 Ford Taurus LX Sedan

1987 Ford Taurus LX interior

1987 Ford Escort GL 4-door Hatchback

1987 Ford Escort GL interior

1987 Ford LTD Crown Victoria LX Sedan

1987 Ford LTD Crown Victoria LX interior

1987 Ford Tempo All-Wheel Drive 4-door Sedan

1987 Ford Tempo LX interior

1987 Ford EXP Sport Coupe

Those 80s Cars - Ford

1987 - LINCOLN

Last Model Run: 1987 Lincoln Continental Givenchy Edition

1987 Lincoln Mark VII LSC

1987 Lincoln Mark VII interior

1987 Lincoln Town Car Cartier edition

1987 - MERCURY

1987 Mercury Sable GS Sedan

> Sable drops 2.5 liter engine, standard engine is 3.0 liter V6

1987 Mercury Sable GS Wagon

1987 Mercury Grand Marquis Colony Park

1987 Mercury Grand Marquis LS Sedan

Last Model Run: 1987 Mercury Lynx Wagon

1987 Mercury Sable LS interior

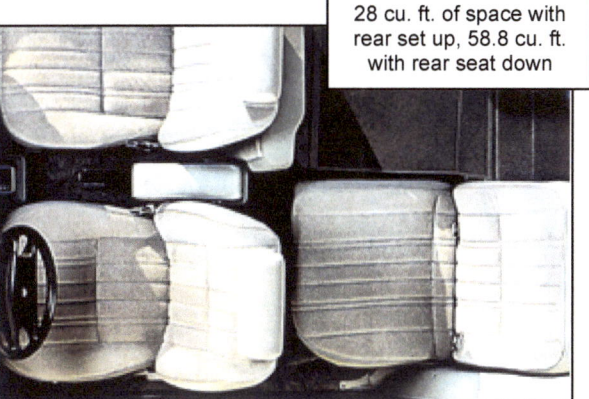

> 28 cu. ft. of space with rear set up, 58.8 cu. ft. with rear seat down

1987 Mercury Lynx GS wagon interior

Refreshed: 1987 Mercury Cougar

Refreshed: 1987 Mercury Cougar & XR-7 (right)

1987 Mercury Cougar LS interior

1987 Mercury Topaz LS 4-door Sedan

1987 Mercury Topaz LS interior

1987 Mercury Cougar XR-7 electronic instrumentation

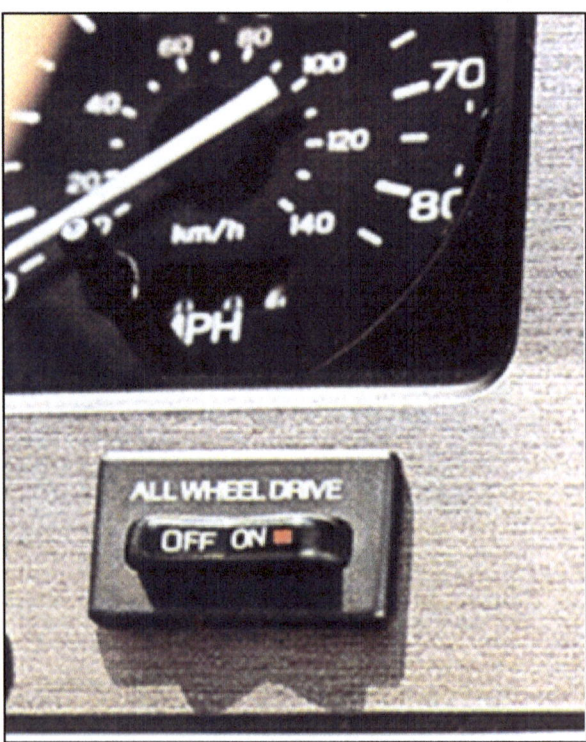
1987 Mercury Topaz All-Wheel Drive option

Those 80s Cars - Ford

1987 - MERKUR

0-60 in 7.8 seconds

1987 Merkur XR4Ti

1987 Merkur XR4Ti

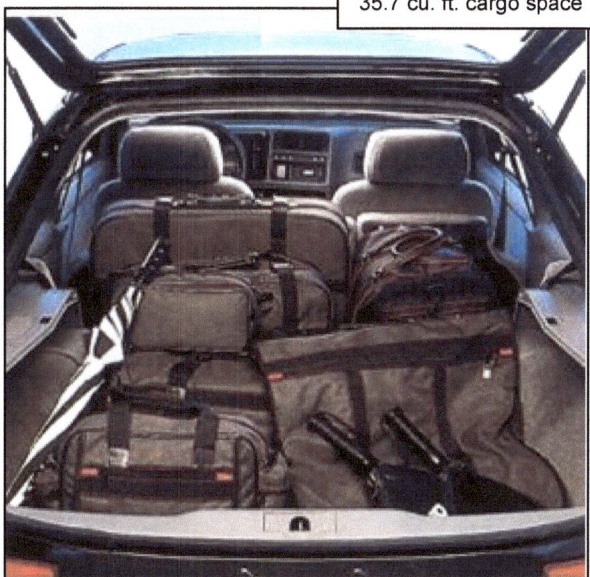

35.7 cu. ft. cargo space

1987 Merkur XR4Ti with rear seats folded provide 35.7 cu. ft. of space

1987 Merkur XR4Ti interior

1987 Merkur XR4Ti instrument panel

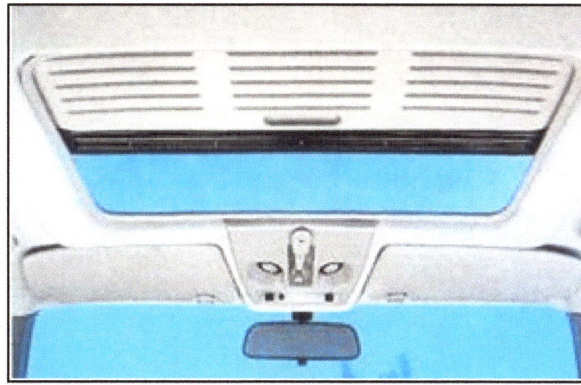

1987 Merkur XR4Ti optional moonroof

From the Brochure: "Merkur XR4Ti. The performance coupe from Germany that is advancing the art of driving. It is from a country where the speed limit is often regulated only by the driver's skill and the automobile's design. Where the switchbacks of a narrow mountain road challenge both driver and machine. The XR4Ti sport coupe is the product of that attitude, an automobile for the kind of driver who would go a few miles out of the way to discover that 'perfect' road." – 1987 Merkur XR4Ti

1988

1988 Facts at Glance

News Headlines

- Iran/Iraq war ends
- Terrorist blow up Pan Am jet over Lockerbie
- Hubble space telescope placed in orbit
- Stealth bomber unveiled

Tops in Pop Culture

Music
- Faith, George Michael

Movies
- Rain Man

TV Show
- The Cosby Show

Sports Champions

Basketball
- L.A. Lakers

Football
- Washington Redskins

Baseball
- L.A. Dodgers

Motor Trend – Car of the Year

Pontiac Grand Prix

Those 80s Cars - Ford

1988 - FORD

5.0 liter V8 & AOD

1988 Ford Thunderbird Sport

1988 Ford Thunderbird Turbo Coupe interior

1988 Ford Mustang GT

1988 Ford Mustang GT interior

New 3.8 liter V6 option

1988 Ford Taurus LX sedan

1988 Ford Taurus LX instrument panel

1988 Ford Taurus LX interior

1988 Ford Escort GT 2-door Hatchback

1988 Ford EXP Luxury Coupe

1988 Ford Escort GT interior

New Model: 1988 Ford Festiva

1.3 liter 4-cylinder w/ 4- & 5-speed manuals & 3-speed auto

Refreshed: 1988 Ford Tempo GL

1988 Ford Tempo instrument panel

Refreshed: 1988 Ford LTD Crown Victoria 4-door Sedan

Refreshed: 1988 Ford LTD Country Squire Wagon

1988 LTD Crown Victoria is refreshed with updated front and rear end styling

1988 Ford LTD Crown Victoria LX interior

Those 80s Cars - Ford

1988 - LINCOLN

1988 Lincoln Continental Town Car

1988 Lincoln Town Car interior

1988 Lincoln Continental instrument panel

1988 Lincoln Continental cloth interior

1988 Lincoln Mark VII LSC

1988 Lincoln Mark VII LSC interior

1988 Lincoln Town Car

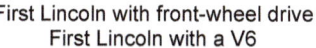
First Lincoln with front-wheel drive
First Lincoln with a V6

New Model: 1988 Lincoln Continental

New Model: 1988 Lincoln Continental

.35 drag

3.8 liter (232) V6
4-speed AOD

New Model: 1988 Lincoln Continental

1988 Lincoln Continental interior with optional leather seating

1988 - MERCURY

5.0 liter V8 & AOD on XR-7 models

1988 Mercury Cougar XR-7

1988 Mercury Cougar XR-7 analog instruments

New Model: 1988 Mercury Tracer 2-door Hatchback

1988 Mercury Tracer LS interior

New Model: 1988 Mercury Tracer LS 4-door Hatchback

Tracers feature a 1.6 liter OHC multi-port electronic fuel injected 4-cylinder engine

New Model: 1988 Mercury Tracer LS Wagon

73   Those 80s Cars - Ford

New 3.8 liter V6 option

Refreshed: 1988 Mercury Topaz XR5 2-door & LTS 4-door

1988 Mercury Sable GS Sedan

1988 Mercury Topaz LS interior

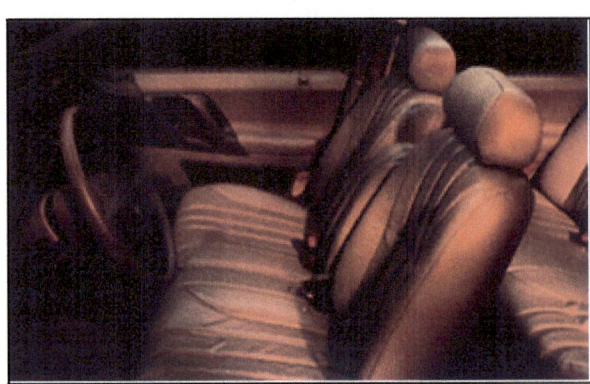

1988 Mercury Sable LS leather interior

1988 Mercury Grand Marquis Colony Park

1988 Mercury Grand Marquis LS

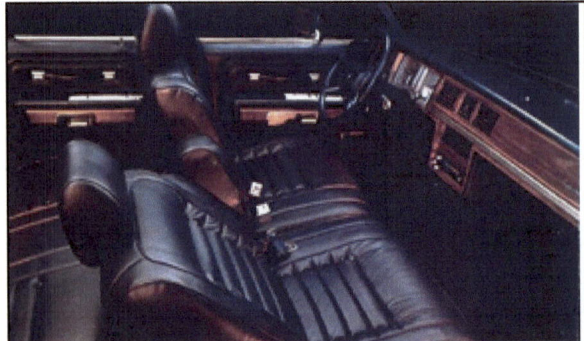

1988 Mercury Grand Marquis LS leather interior

1988 Mercury Grand Marquis LS cloth interior

1988 - MERKUR

1988 Merkur XR4Ti

2.9 liter V6, 140 hp

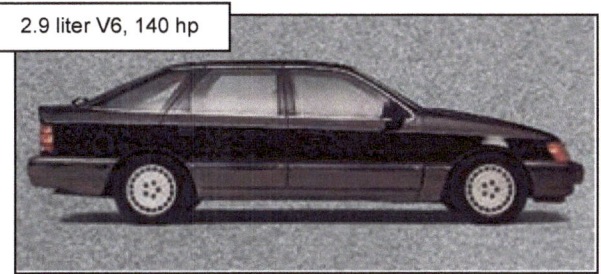
New Model: 1988 Merkur Scorpio 4-door Hatchback

1988 Merkur XR4Ti optional leather interior

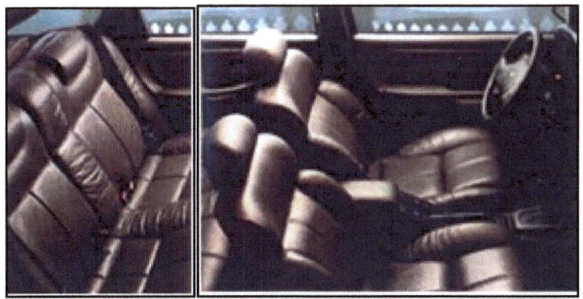
1988 Merkur Scorpio interior with optional leather

From the Brochure: "All the performance of a fine German sedan, but with a major difference. Exceptional interior comfort. Scorpio's interior appointments and obvious attention to personal comfort separate it from all other German sedans in an exceptional manner."
- 1988 Merkur Scorpio

5-speed manual & 4-speed automatic transmission availability

New Model: 1988 Merkur Scorpio 4-door Hatchback

1989

1989 - Facts at Glance

News Headlines

- USSR pulls out of Afghanistan
- George Bush Sr inaugurated as President
- Exxon Valdez spills 240,000 barrels of oil
- Leona Helmsley convicted on tax fraud
- Ford buys Jaguar
- Berlin Wall comes down

Tops in Pop Culture

Music
- Look Away, Chicago

Movies
- Batman

TV Show
- Roseanne

Sports Champions

Basketball
- Detroit Pistons

Football
- San Francisco 49ers

Baseball
- Oakland A's

Motor Trend – Car of the Year

Ford Thunderbird SC

Those 80s Cars - Ford

1989 - FORD

New Model: 1989 Ford Thunderbird Super Coupe

4-wheel anti-lock brakes, Automatic Ride Control suspension, super-charged intercooled 3.8 liter V6 & 5-speed manual

1989 Ford Thunderbird LX interior

1989 Ford Mustang GT Hatchback

1989 Ford Mustang LX Coupe

New Series: 1989 Ford Taurus SHO

3.0 liter V6, 4 valves per cylinder, DOHC, 220hp with 5-speed manual transmission only

1989 Ford Taurus LX instrument panel

2.2 liter 4-cylinder, with turbo option

New Model: 1989 Ford Probe GT

1989 Ford Probe instrument panel

5-speed manual & 4-speed automatic

1989 Ford Probe interior

1989 Ford Tempo AWD

1989 Ford Festiva

1989 Ford Tempo LX interior

1989 Ford Escort LX Wagon

3 Escort series: Pony, LX & GT

1989 Ford Escort GT

1989 Ford Tempo GLS instrument panel

1989 Ford Escort instrument panel

From the Brochure: "Escort features front-wheel drive, electronic fuel-injected performance, 4-wheel independent suspension and an interior environment designed to be both comfortable and practical."
- 1989 Ford Escort

1989 Ford LTD Crown Victoria

1989 Ford LTD Crown Victoria LX interior

Those 80s Cars - Ford

1989 - LINCOLN

Continental is first domestic car with standard driver and passenger front air bags

1989 Lincoln Mark VII LSC

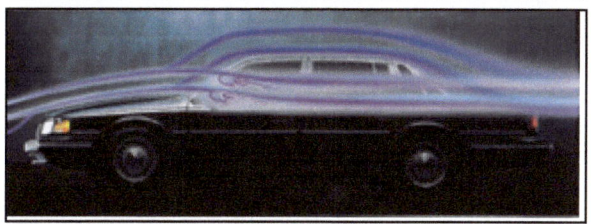
1989 Lincoln Continental

1989 Lincoln Mark VII LSC instrument panel

Last Model Run: 1989 Lincoln Town Car

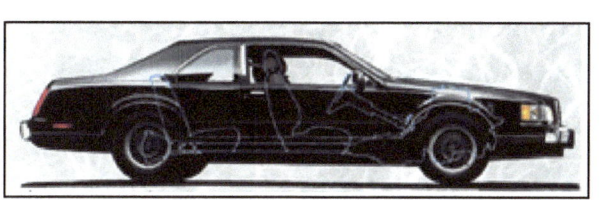

1989 Lincoln Town Car Cartier interior

1989 - MERCURY

1989 Mercury Sedan Line

1989 Mercury Tracer 4-door Hatchback

1989 Mercury Sable LS

1989 Mercury Sable LS

1989 Mercury Sable LS optional leather interior

1989 Mercury Tracer interior

68 standard features

New Model: 1989 Mercury Cougar XR7

After many years being badged as "XR-7", in 1989, the dash is dropped and it is now badged "XR7"

1989 Mercury Cougar XR7 instrument panel

Standard Cougar models come with a 3.8 liter V6 producing 140 horsepower at 3,800 RPM

1989 Mercury Cougar LS interior

1989 Mercury Topaz

1989 Mercury Topaz LS Sedan

1989 Mercury Topaz LTS interior

From the Brochure: "Cougar XR7. Comfort just got a shot of adrenaline. The objective was to combine comfort and control with uncommon quickness. The result is the new Cougar XR7. Its adrenaline takes the form of a 210-horsepower supercharged V-6 with intercooler. It delivers load of performance that will draw more than just a passing glance from enthusiasts."
- 1989 Mercury Cougar XR7

1989 Mercury Wagons: Tracer, Grand Marquis Colony Park and Sable LS

1989 Mercury Grand Marquis

1989 Mercury Grand Marquis LS interior

From the Brochure: "Mercury Grand Marquis. Comfort and control on a grand scale. Grand Marquis is one automobile that doesn't ask its driver or passengers to compromise. Its interior possess more room than 99 percent of today's automobiles. There's body-on-frame construction and the control that comes with a V-8 engine, power brakes, nitrogen gas-pressurized shocks and a four-speed automatic transmission.

Grand Marquis sedans and Colony Park wagons are available with a number of additional comfort and convenience features. In addition to the standard electronic AM/FM stereo radio with four speakers there are three other radio options. You may wish to consider the high-level electronic AM stereo/FM stereo cassette audio system with a power amplifier and six speakers.

Both sedans and wagons can be ordered with the Trailer Tow III option."
- 1989 Mercury Grand Marquis

1989 - MERKUR

Last Model Run: 1989 Merkur XR4Ti

Last Model Run: 1989 Merkur Scorpio Sedan & XR4Ti Coupe

From the Brochure: "The bold, rakish design of the XR4Ti promises a driving experience that is clearly a cut above the norm. And on the road, the XR4Ti fulfills that promise with a striking combination of performance and comfort."
 - 1989 MerkurXR4Ti

1989 Merkur XR4Ti standard cloth interior

1989 Merkur XR4Ti optional leather interior

Those 80s Cars - Ford

Table of Contents	2
Foreword	3
The 80's Measured	4
1980	5
1980 - Facts at Glance	5
1980 - FORD	6
1980 - LINCOLN	9
1980 - MERCURY	11
1981	14
1981 - Facts at Glance	14
1981 - FORD	15
1981 - LINCOLN	18
1981 - MERCURY	21
1982	23
1982 - Facts at Glance	23
1982 - FORD	24
1982 - LINCOLN	27
1982 - MERCURY	29
1983	32
1983 - Facts at Glance	32
1983 - FORD	33
1983 - LINCOLN	35
1983 - MERCURY	36
1984	38
1984 - Facts at Glance	38
1984 - FORD	39
1984 - LINCOLN	42
1984 - MERCURY	44
1985	46
1985 - Facts at Glance	46
1985 - FORD	47
1985 - LINCOLN	49
1985 - MERCURY	50
1985 - MERKUR	52
1986	53
1986 - Facts at Glance	53
1986 - FORD	54
1986 - LINCOLN	57
1986 - MERCURY	58
1986 - MERKUR	60
1987	61
1987- Facts at Glance	61
1987 - FORD	62
1987 - LINCOLN	64
1987 - MERCURY	65
1987 - MERKUR	67
1988	68
1988 Facts at Glance	68
1988 - FORD	69
1988 - LINCOLN	71
1988 - MERCURY	73
1988 - MERKUR	75
1989	76
1989 - Facts at Glance	76
1989 - FORD	77
1989 - LINCOLN	79
1989 - MERCURY	80
1989 - MERKUR	83